SIX WORD
LESSONS

FOR DADS WITH
AUTISTIC KIDS

100 Lessons

to

Help Fathers and their Children
Create Strong Bonds

Lonnie Pacelli

GrowingUpAutistic.com

Six-Word Lessons for Dads with Autistic Kids – 6wordlessons.com

Editing by Patty Pacelli

Published by Pacelli Publishing
9905 Lake Washington Blvd. NE, #D-103
Bellevue, Washington 98004
Pacellipublishing.com

ISBN-10: 1-933750-35-9
ISBN-13: 978-1-933750-35-4

Trevor was born December 1, 1992. By all accounts he appeared to be just like any other baby. His big sister, Briana, is two and one-half years older than Trevor and set the standard for us as to what life with children would be like. At age two Briana was speaking in full sentences, while Trevor at age two was barely saying any words. Briana demanded almost constant attention from my wife, Patty and I, while Trevor preferred to play by himself. Trevor went to speech therapy and then to a special preschool for children with disabilities or behavioral issues. At age five we took him to the University of Washington Autism Center where they tested him and diagnosed him with Autism Spectrum Disorder (ASD) in the category of Pervasive Developmental Disorder – Not Otherwise Specified (PDD-NOS). There it was, we had an autistic child.

As parents we were not at all prepared for life with an ASD child. Patty was a stay-at-home mom and became well versed in how to relate to Trevor; I, not nearly as much as Patty. While I did figure some things out, I made a lot of mistakes as a father that if I got a mulligan would never do again. That's why I wrote **Six-Word Lessons for Dads with Autistic Kids**.

In **Six-Word Lessons for Dads with Autistic Kids**, you'll get 100 concise, simple-to-understand lessons written in "man-speak" to help fathers get nuggets quickly and efficiently. Some may apply to your situation, some may not. My hope, though, is you'll be able to implement a few of these nuggets to help you build a stronger bond with your child.

I'd love to hear your thoughts on this book and how any of the lessons have helped or not helped you. Tell us your story at www.growingupautistic.com.

Table of Contents

Definitions and Reasons for this Book 7

Cues your Child May Have ASD 19

Will He Ever Amount to Anything? 31

My Spouse and I Don't Agree 41

Why Doesn't He Like Normal Things? 49

Helping with Reading, Writing, and Arithmetic 61

Disciplining Can Have Very Unintended Consequences 71

He's Not You, Get Over it 81

Find Things to Get Interested In 89

Get Him to Try New Things 99

Don't Underestimate His Life Skills Abilities 107

Remember You Have Other Kids Too 115

The Journey Doesn't End, it Changes 121

Definitions and Reasons for this Book

1

There are three types of ASDs.

Autism Spectrum Disorders (ASDs) come in three forms: autistic disorder (also known as "classic autism"), Asperger Syndrome, and Pervasive Developmental Disorder – Not Otherwise Specified (PDD-NOS, also known as "atypical autism").

2

Autistic Disorder – the most typical ASD.

Autistic Disorder is what comes to mind when most envision someone with autism. Significant language delays, unusual interests, and social and communication challenges are common. Many also have intellectual disability.

3

Asperger Syndrome – milder Autism Spectrum Disorder.

People with Asperger Syndrome typically have social challenges and unusual, obsessive behaviors and interests. However, they usually do not have intellectual disability or language delay issues.

4

Pervasive Developmental Disorder-Not Otherwise Specified.

People with PDD-NOS often have fewer and milder symptoms than those with Autistic Disorder. Communication and social challenges are generally prevalent.

5

ASDs account for 2% of births

The Center for Disease Control (CDC) estimates are that one in 50 people between the ages of six and seventeen have ASD. This number is up from one in 88 surveyed in 2007.

6

Boys have ASD more than girls.

According to an extensive CDC study conducted in 2008, boys are five times more likely than girls to have Autism Spectrum Disorder.

7

There's no one cause of ASD.

Some potential causes linked to ASD are having a sibling or parent with ASD, taking thalidomide or valproic acid during pregnancy and some genetic disorders. There is no one definitive cause as to why someone is born with ASD.

8

Unproven causes of Autism Spectrum Disorder.

Vaccines, tantrums, junk food, bad parenting, television, stressful family situations, or cell phones have not been reliably proven to cause ASD. While there may be other results from these factors, ASD has not been proven to be linked to any of them.

9

The lessons you'll be reading about.

The experiences you will read in the rest of this book apply predominantly to those with PDD-NOS and Aspergers, as this is where our first-hand parental experience with ASD lies. However, many of the lessons included will apply to those with autistic disorder as well. My hope is you pick up several nuggets to help you in your journey as the father of an ASD child.

10

The people you'll be reading about.

There are three people I will refer to in this book. Patty is my wonderful wife and is very active in ASD awareness. Briana is our eldest and is a nurse. Trevor is our youngest and desires a career in film. Trevor was diagnosed with PDD-NOS at age five. The experiences you'll read about revolve around us as a family and our journey with ASD.

11

I screwed up
way too much.

I didn't write this book because I did everything right in being a father to Trevor. In fact, I did a *lot* of things wrong in my parenting. I wasn't nearly as sensitive as I needed to be when it came to accommodating a child with ASD. My one goal is to help other fathers of an ASD child avoid some of the same mistakes I made.

Cues your Child May Have ASD

12

They may have very obsessive interests.

From very early on, Trevor showed obsessive interests in certain things. At age two it was puzzles. At age five it was the television show *Blues Clues*. Throughout his childhood he was obsessed with drawing just about anything. He still has strong interests such as movies (fortunately that is his chosen profession) but is not nearly as obsessive as when he was younger.

13

They just want to be alone.

Many with ASD are perfectly content being on their own, focused on their favorite activities. This can be perplexing, particularly when the autistic child has siblings who like interaction. Briana was a very social child who craved interaction. Trevor was the polar opposite. As an adult he still needs his alone time.

14

They avoid looking into your eyes.

Those with ASD typically avoid eye contact. With Trevor, we found that it wasn't that he disliked eye contact, it was just something he didn't normally do. Patty and I consciously worked with him to look us in the eye when talking. As an adult he mostly establishes and engages in eye contact during conversations.

15

They have difficulty expressing their feelings.

Many with ASD have difficulty verbalizing feelings of happiness, sadness, anger, etc. You can definitely see through their actions how they are feeling, but they are less likely to verbalize it. Trevor as an adult still has difficulty with this at times and gets frustrated with himself when he can't verbalize his feelings.

23

16

They don't read other people well.

Because those with ASD are so into their own world and are very literal by nature, they have difficulty "reading" other people and observing social cues like facial expressions, moods, or tone of voice. Trevor had a lot of difficulty with this growing up but has grown more aware of social cues as an adult. For example, he now understands sarcasm and will say, "that's sarcasm right?"

17

They have peculiar repetitive body movements.

Some with ASD may flap their hands, run in circles, or do some other body movement. Trevor would rock from side to side in bed before going to sleep. This started with birth and continued into his early elementary years. He would also run in circles in the living room and talk to himself, which seemed to calm him.

18

They need to keep a schedule.

Having the ability to keep to a schedule is important to someone with ASD. You could set your watch to some things Trevor did during the day, like setting the dinner table (5:50 p.m.), walking on the treadmill (6:30 p.m.), or having an evening snack (8:00 p.m.). We consequently kept a very orderly and predictable house and all four of us grew very comfortable with schedules.

19

Even fun surprises can wreak havoc.

So what kid doesn't like hearing, "Hey, let's go out for ice cream!" While many kids would gleefully run for the car, those with ASD could find it difficult because it is an unplanned activity that wasn't expected. We learned to not spring unplanned activities of any kind on Trevor; we would give him advance notice so he could incorporate the activity into his schedule.

20

Trying new things isn't very fun.

Whether it be new foods, new activities, or different clothes, doing something new takes the person with ASD out of his familiar routine and disrupts his plans. With food, we had an agreement with Trevor that he had to try something ten times before he decided he didn't like it. Had we not done this, he might still be eating hot dogs, grilled cheese, or macaroni and cheese for nearly every meal.

21

They have delayed speech and language.

Those with ASD typically lag in speech and language progression. When Trevor was two years old he was barely saying 10 words, which was a stark contrast to Briana, who was rifling off entire sentences by age two. His comprehension was also delayed. He began private speech and language therapy at age two to help him interact using words.

22

Their senses are much more sensitive.

Senses such as smells, sounds, and touch are more sensitive in people with ASD, and they can be much more amplified, causing sometimes severe and unusual reactions. Trevor is sensitive to loud noises, and in elementary school he wore headphones at events such as school assemblies to drown out the high noise levels. As an adult, he is more tolerant, but still gets agitated at unexpected or sudden loud noises.

Will He Ever Amount to Anything?

23

What is your definition of "anything"?

As fathers, we innately have visions of our newborn children being the next Einstein, Lincoln, or Gehrig. Discovering your child has ASD can feel like cold water being thrown on your expectations. Raising a child with ASD means being more open to what success will look like for your child and realigning your expectations of him.

24

Will he be able to drive?

While some people with ASD do not learn to drive, many are actually excellent drivers. Trevor had difficulty with the written test, so he was allowed to take the test with audio headphones as well as the usual video, which helped him to pass. He passed the driving portion on the first try and got his license at 16. His driving instructor's only criticism was that he sometimes "drove too slow." That would be music to any parent's ears!

25

Can he take care of himself?

From the time he was a toddler, we let Trevor do as much as possible for himself, such as dressing and making breakfast, just as we did with Briana. He was probably ahead of the average child in many areas, and always loved being independent. We gave him instruction where needed, but always expected him to do things for himself. This served him well as he grew up and he is now living on his own in a college residence hall.

26

Will he get married some day?

Many with ASD are happily married and have found the perfect mate to share their life with. Trevor has the desire to be married someday but is not preoccupied with the notion. He is more focused on working toward a successful career in the film industry.

27

Will his children also have ASD?

Given that there is one no clear cause of ASD, it's difficult to say whether or not a parent with ASD will have children with ASD. One of Trevor's teachers in college has Aspergers and has a child with Aspergers and one non-ASD child. The more important question is whether your child wants and is capable of being a parent; not whether your child will have a child with ASD.

28

Will he ever have any friends?

Making friends was certainly one of Trevor's major challenges growing up. Up until he was in ninth grade, he had a few casual friends, but didn't have a strong desire to make or have friends. The older he got, the more he wanted friends, but it was always difficult to form those friendships. He still struggles in this area, but has made great strides at learning skills and making the effort to make and maintain friendships.

29

Will kids make
fun of him?

This was very painful for us. Yes, other kids did make fun of Trevor and knew what buttons to push to get him agitated. Others who he thought were friends turned out to be mean kids who took advantage of his ASD. He saw a therapist during high school to help him with some of his struggles.

30

Will he ever have a job?

Having ASD doesn't mean your child will be forever unable to work. Trevor got his first job after high school working at a summer camp. He subsequently worked at our church doing maintenance work while in college. We were amazed at what he was able to do and his employers loved his promptness, willingness to do any job, and his being "all business" when at work.

31

Will he always need our help?

When we compare Trevor's with Briana's "neediness indexes," both still need us for different things. Trevor needs a bit more coaching on new life skills events, such as signing up for college classes for the first time. We are very deliberate in establishing our parental role as coaches and tell him, "Our job is to tell you what we think, your job is to decide what to do with it."

My Spouse and I Don't Agree

32

One knows more than the other.

It's likely that one of you will have done more research on ASDs and techniques to use in parenting your child. It's super important you both get well versed on the basics of ASDs (this book is a good start), that you do some of your own research, and you recommend reading to each other to help you get up to speed.

33

One doesn't believe he has ASD.

I've met a number of parents where one spouse was in denial about an ASD diagnosis for their child. This is quite simply a recipe for disaster. If necessary, get a second opinion but be proactive in taking steps to ensure you both align on the ASD diagnosis.

34

One is overprotective and shelters him.

In our experience, it has been good to have some healthy tension, with Patty being more protective and me wanting Trevor to fend for himself. Either one of us working alone might have erred to one extreme or the other. If you differ in this area, embrace the difference and look for common ground.

35

One wants to make him normal.

At the writing of this book there is no known cure for any of the Autism Spectrum Disorders. You have to work together based on a goal of supporting your child with ASD, not trying to cure him of it. You'll have much greater success if you adopt a mindset of acceptance.

36

One doesn't want to be involved.

In my opinion, having one parent shoulder the full weight of caring for and nurturing an ASD child while the other plays the role of non-existent parent is worse than a single person raising an ASD child on his or her own. The involved parent has enough on his or her plate without having to deal with an apathetic spouse. If there are two parents, ensure both are involved.

37

Grandparents have different points of view.

You may have parents who feel obligated to give their opinion on how you should be raising your ASD child. Watch out for conflicting or uninformed opinions which drive a wedge between you and your spouse, particularly if there is no prior experience with ASD. Accept their opinion then together with your spouse decide what to do with it.

Why Doesn't He Like Normal Things?

38

Beware some sports will frustrate him.

We signed Trevor up for soccer when he was four. When on the field he would stand there and cry. What we learned was that the randomness of play and the yelling by parents and other kids was too much for him to take. We found more orderly sports like baseball and tennis to be more palatable to him, though he was never really passionate about either playing or watching sports.

39

Vacations can throw him off schedule.

On our first day at Walt Disney World, Trevor told us at 3 p.m. that we needed to go back to the hotel room so he could watch *Blues Clues*. We were in a place all kids love, but he didn't want to break his routine. As he got older we convinced him that when we were on vacation there was no routine, so his "vacation" routine was that everything would be different, which he was OK with.

40

Recess isn't all fun and games.

Because Trevor craves order in his life, the randomness, yelling and other activity at recess was frustrating for him. While other kids may love the activity and stimulation, a child with ASD may very well see it as stressful and confusing.

41

Surprises aren't such a good idea.

Some people with ASD can be so lost in their own world that they are incredibly sensitive to anything unexpected. Surprises such as sneaking behind their back to intentionally startle them or other teasing usually upsets them.

42

He really needs some time alone.

Briana loves being around people most of the time. Being around people for extended periods of time gets exhausting for Trevor. Even around family members or people he likes, he needs to have time to get away by himself. In college Trevor was able to get a private dorm room so he could safely retreat to a place he always knew he could be alone.

43

What kid doesn't like drinking soda?

The first time Trevor took a sip of soda he puked all over the table (and of course we were in a restaurant). He also didn't eat his first cheeseburger until he was nine. Some foods that most kids love might not appeal to a child with ASD.

44

Joking can be no laughing matter.

Because people with ASD have difficulty discerning between seriousness and joking, some may be confused, offended, or hurt by what may seem to be a harmless joke. As Trevor has gotten older he's been better about jokes, but still gets hurt if a joke is directed at him.

45

Hugs can be uncomfortable or painful.

With his heightened sensitivity to touch, Trevor didn't particularly enjoy being hugged as a toddler or adolescent. Over time, he has learned that hugging is an acceptable social norm. As an adult, if we don't see him for more than a couple of days Trevor will gladly give us a brief hug along with a big "Hi!"

46

Sleepovers weren't very fun for him.

Sleepovers (either staying at another house or having a friend over) meant a change in routine and not being able to do the things Trevor typically got to do on his own. When he did stay at another house for the night we gave him plenty of warning and ensured he had time by himself to avoid getting frustrated with too many people around.

47

He can't explain what's bothering him.

Trevor may have something that is bothering him, but at times he finds it difficult to put his feelings into words. If Patty or I ask him what's wrong, sometimes he'll tell us that something is wrong but he doesn't know how to put it into words.

Helping with Reading, Writing, and Arithmetic

48

To homeschool or not to homeschool.

Patty and I decided to partially homeschool Trevor for seventh and eighth grades, then he returned to public school from ninth grade on. Homeschooling was helpful because it gave him more focused help than he would have received in public school. The downside was that he didn't get as much social interaction. Looking back, we believe we made the right decision to homeschool for those crucial years.

49

What were your strongest school subjects?

My stronger subjects were math and science, while Patty's were language arts and humanities. We divvied up homework and homeschool responsibilities by those topic areas to give Trevor the best quality of education and homework assistance. He also attended a homeschool learning center part-time, which was a valuable support.

50

Don't force your strengths on him.

While math and science were my stronger suit, I was dealing with a child who didn't enjoy either of those topics. Trevor and I would both get frustrated with each other when he wasn't getting something that I thought he should be getting. I wanted him to do well in those subjects because I did well in those subjects. Man was I wrong.

51

Professional tutors can help big time.

Trevor was fortunate enough to have some dedicated tutoring assistance in a couple of his classes. This was tremendous in that it wasn't mom or dad doing the tutoring and the tutor was much closer to the content and learning methods being used in school. It was extremely helpful.

52

What is an
IEP all about?

In the United States the Individuals with Disabilities Education Act (IDEA) mandates that children with disabilities be put on an Individualized Education Plan (IEP). Some may see this as bureaucracy at work; I saw it as a great way to partner with the school to ensure the best possible instruction. You must know about your child's IEP and be actively involved in its execution.

53

Encourage involvement in social groups.

Trevor has always loved the arts and in middle school joined the drama club, which continued through high school. He was involved both onstage as a performer and offstage doing various jobs such as props and set decoration. His experience in drama was significant in helping him shape his social skills and learn how to interact with peers.

54

Partner with the teachers and administrators.

We learned early on that having a regular dialogue with Trevor's teachers, counselors, and administrators was huge in helping to ensure the best possible learning experience which would lead to Trevor's success. Even during our two years of homeschooling, we utilized the public school system for courses, counseling, speech therapy, and IEP assistance.

55

Be aware of the potential bully.

It's no joke that kids can be mean, and an ASD child can be even more susceptible to bullying. As a parent, it's important to work actively with the school system on any bullying incidents and to reinforce with your child that he has done nothing wrong if innocent. He already is likely feeling angry over the incident; you'll make it worse if you are anything less than supportive with him.

56

Accommodations don't stop after high school.

Trevor went to a community college for two years after high school. We saw that as a great stepping stone for him. The college has a very active ASD support program headed by a director with Aspergers. He then transferred to a four-year university with an active disability resource center where he was allowed accommodations such as a private dorm room and ability to take tests in a room by himself.

Disciplining Can Have Very Unintended Consequences

57

Don't ever discipline out of anger.

Sure, this is something a parent should practice with any child. With Trevor, whenever I would get angry with him, any negative feelings he had would be amplified and replayed over and over in his mind. It affected him much more than it did Briana and he still can vividly recall whenever I was angry at him. This one I'll regret for the rest of my life.

58

He must know when he's wrong.

Regardless of ASD, the child must learn right from wrong to the extent he is capable of understanding, and recognize there are consequences when misbehaving. Be careful about being too accommodating and not correcting wrong behavior because of his ASD.

59

Alignment with your spouse is crucial.

Patty and I weren't always aligned when it came to disciplining either Briana or Trevor. This not only created stress with the kids, it created stress between us. Be deliberate about putting a discipline game plan together and stick with it.

60

Raising your voice exacerbates the problem.

I came from a family of yellers who would raise their voices when angry. Because of this, the idea of raising one's voice when disciplining seemed natural to me, so that's what I did. For Trevor, raising my voice coupled with his sensitivity to sound was like nails on a blackboard to him. It was not the right method and didn't help at all.

61

Find ways to discipline without agitating.

We used a couple of techniques which worked well. One was losing a privilege, such as their usual bedtime reading and music cassettes (my kids remember this as "no book and no tape"). The other was getting "work chips" where they got a poker chip which represented an extra household task like emptying the dishwasher. Both worked well to get the point across.

62

Don't show favorites when disciplining them.

When siblings are in the picture, be careful not to let your child with ASD get away with some things that the siblings would not get away with. The siblings will sniff out the unfairness in discipline and be resentful of the child with ASD. At the same time, the child with ASD may also see that he can get away with more things and take advantage of you.

63

Being blunt isn't reason to discipline.

Many people with ASD are extremely blunt and direct in their conversation. With Trevor, I characterize it as, "Trevor just says what everyone else is thinking or wants to say." While he might have come across as rude, he wasn't misbehaving--it's simply how he's naturally wired. Use those times as calm teaching moments to help him learn and not as opportunities to discipline.

64

Tell him that you love him.

Disciplining can be confusing for any child, especially when disciplining out of anger. For a child with ASD, the feelings get amplified and he can take any discipline as a sign that he is a bad person or that you hate him. Make sure he knows you love him and that discipline is about correcting behavior, not about withholding love.

He's Not You, Get Over it

65

You live yours, he lives his.

First and foremost, you need to accept and embrace that your ASD child may be interested in much, some, or none of what you are interested in. You may have envisioned your child being a star sports figure, a power CEO, or a famous actor. That's all really nice, but it doesn't matter. As with any child, he needs to discover and follow his own passion.

66

But I see so much potential!

True, there might be the potential for your ASD child to do something great. Force it on him and you're sure to cause him to run the other way. It could just be that his passion needs to grow into his potential. Give him time and space to do it.

67

How about we watch some football?

I can make this statement and get an immediate "Sure, Dad!", but it comes from Briana. She'll watch game after game with me. Trevor has no interest in watching football or any kind of sports with me. As much as I'd like for both my kids to watch football, I am very content with the other activities Trevor and I enjoy together, like watching movies and eating at Old Country Buffet.

68

Maybe he'll follow me into business.

I love business and the challenge of creating something that others want and will pay for. Trevor loves creating things, but not for profit motive. He loves the artistic side of creating things and couldn't care less about the "business" side of things. He's not passionate about it and probably never will be.

69

I walked five miles to school...

Every father has stories about how his kids have life so much easier than he did. While it's good to remind your ASD child of the luxuries that he has in life, it's not cool to make him feel guilty about it. Remember people with ASD tend to amplify things, so what may seem minor to you could be like the end of the world to him.

70

Tell him how you've messed up.

Trevor loves to hear that his dad is human, that he's made mistakes, and that he's willing to admit his mistakes to his son. A number of times when talking through a mistake Trevor has made I'll tell him a story of how I really screwed something up. He loves to hear that his old man has done some dumb stuff (correction: a *lot* of dumb stuff) and that I'm willing to admit it to him. It's very therapeutic for both of us.

71

Remind him of his own strengths.

Trevor likes it when I praise strengths particularly when his strengths are my weaknesses, for example, his drawing skill. When he was younger, we would play a restaurant game while waiting for dinner. I would ask him to draw what the baby would look like if two characters (say Goofy and Minnie) got married and had a baby. The drawings were amazing. I on the other hand can't even draw stick figures.

Find Things to Get Interested In

72

What TV shows does he watch?

With Trevor, it was easy to know which TV shows he liked to watch. He talked about them. We started watching a few TV shows together and took to recording them so we could watch them right after dinner. It gave us an opportunity to talk about the TV show and weave in other conversations around the show.

73

What movies are interesting to him?

Men in Black. Trevor and I both love that movie and have seen it dozens of times. We also did quite a few visits to the theater to see movies. Some were great, some not so great. The point is that going to and watching movies is something that he and I do together and has helped in our bonding as father and son.

74

Does he talk about any hobbies?

With an ASD child it is usually pretty easy to hone in on his interests. He'll do it all the time and/or talk about it constantly. Watch to see what things he is interested in and do some parallel play together, then use it as a means to talk about things with him.

75

Favorite restaurants help with creating bonds.

Growing up, Trevor had some favorite places to eat. When he was a toddler it was McDonalds. Later it became Old Country Buffet, now it's The Melting Pot. We also enjoy going to breakfast together and now whenever we're with my father-in-law he expects that we're going to go out to breakfast together. It's just part of the routine.

76

Make sure it becomes scheduled time.

Trevor's and my special activities are almost always scheduled in some way. For things we would do on a regular basis we would have a set time that we would do it. For special events, it worked best to give him advance notice so he could plan it into his schedule. Don't spring an activity on him last minute, even if it's something he loves to do.

77

Don't interfere with spouse and child.

There are some things that Trevor and I do together, and there are some things that Trevor and Patty do together. Trevor enjoys those times and prefers that Patty and I don't infringe on the other's special time.

78

Be mindful of competing with him.

Trevor is very interested in photography and has an incredible eye for finding amazing shots. I am very supportive of his hobby and genuinely am amazed at his photographic prowess. He wants it to be *his* thing and doesn't want me to go out and buy a camera and take pictures with him. We're completely content going somewhere where he can take great pictures and I watch him at his craft.

79

Parallel play can be very effective.

Trevor and I had a kids game that we would play on the internet where Flintstones characters would do things like have snowball fights. He and I played that game together but did it on two separate computers sitting side by side playing our own games. It was a lot of fun because we got to talk a lot about how we were doing in the game but we also were playing separately.

80

Interact but let him stay focused.

Doing things together means participating in an activity while at the same time sprinkling in conversation and questions. His being engrossed in an activity is like studying for a final; he's very focused on what he's doing and constant interruption is likely to agitate him. Don't overpower him with interaction.

Get Him to
Try New Things

81

You need to help him grow.

Because people with ASD seek comfort in routine, they need help being introduced to new experiences. As a child, Trevor played so well independently that it was easy to just let him do his thing because he was content. However, he needed to grow and develop new routines and interests otherwise he'd stay stuck in neutral.

82

We used a "ten times" technique.

Getting Trevor to try new foods was very difficult. Popcorn, hot dogs, milk, and macaroni and cheese were among his few favorites. Whenever he would try new food, his immediate reaction was that he didn't like it. We used a "ten times" technique where he had to try something ten times before he decided he didn't like it. We weren't militant about enforcement, but it did get him to try new foods and broaden his menu.

83

Let him create routine around it.

Creating a routine around trying new things helps to put something familiar and predictable around something that is not familiar and predictable. Setting an expectation such as, "on Thursdays after dinner we're going to do something we haven't done before" allows him to schedule it in his day and prepare himself for the new activity.

84

Be patient when introducing new things.

As fathers, we tend to want to fix things like repairing a leaky faucet. If you're like me, you also want to see results quickly and feel like, "If I do more then I'll see results faster." Not true with your ASD child. You've got to be patient and not flood him with new things looking for quick results. This is a marathon; you can't run it like a 100-yard dash.

85

Not every new thing will stick.

Just like you may not enjoy every new thing that is sprung on you, don't expect that every new thing you introduce to your child is going to stick. If he's just not interested in the activity after trying it a few times then move on and look for something else to introduce. Remember he's not you; just because you may like something doesn't mean he'll like it.

86

Use numbers when trying new things.

Using a numeric goal worked well with Trevor. Setting a goal like "learn one new thing this summer" and choosing a specific task, made it black and white to him and something he could easily understand. This is much more meaningful than saying, "Try some new things this summer."

87

Work together when introducing new things.

Riding a two-wheeler was a huge accomplishment for Trevor. As a young teenager he still didn't know how to ride a bike, so I was more of the goal-setter of getting him to learn to ride a bike by end of summer and Patty was the teacher who worked with him every day. Her softer style was much more conducive to his learning ability. He did learn to ride and grew to really enjoy it, even riding to school.

Don't Underestimate His Life Skills Abilities

88

He learned to drive a car.

Trevor and Patty practiced driving for hours and hours at school parking lots and in our neighborhood. We also signed Trevor up for private driving lessons to help give him any special attention needed to improve his driving skills. After one of his early driving classes he noticed that our license plate tabs were expired on one of our cars. He not only learned to drive well but saved us a ticket in the process!

89

He manages his own bank account.

When Trevor was 16 we got him a checking account with a debit card and worked with him on the fundamentals of how to use an ATM, how to write a check, and how to check his balance online. His account was linked to ours so we could also monitor what was happening and look for any abnormalities.

90

He uses a credit card responsibly.

When Trevor was 18 we signed him up for a credit card, explained how to use it, including paying his bill online. We explained that he would need to pay it off every month or would start incurring interest charges. We also linked this account to ours to monitor activity. He's never missed a due date and hasn't paid a dime in interest.

91

He made the college deans list.

Trevor has been on the deans list multiple times and has had several quarters where he got all A's in his classes. We saw a big jump in his grades once he learned how to more effectively study by rewriting his notes. The visual and physical action of rewriting notes helped him to better retain information and do better in school.

92

He had chores around the house.

From the time Briana and Trevor were little we gave them chores to do. Trevor had to clean his room and vacuum the stairs. He created a routine of doing them every Sunday around 2:30. Once when Patty's parents were watching the kids for a weekend they were amazed how on Sunday afternoon the kids both did their chores without being asked. Routine has its benefits!

93

He completely takes care of himself.

Now that he is living away from home, Trevor shops for himself, studies on his own, finds his way around, and calls us when he needs help with something. Patty and I instilled self-sufficiency in both Briana and Trevor early in life so he really knows no other way than to take care of himself.

Remember You Have Other Kids Too

94

Make it just something you do.

At home we kept a consistent schedule to create more predictability. For example, we ate dinner at 6:00 every night at the table with no TV or other distractions. It not only helped with predictability but was tremendous for building relationships and keeping in touch with the kids through their teens. Patty and I still dine at 6:00.

95

Do special things with each child.

Briana and I had special traditions that only she and I did. Every Memorial Day weekend, we would do a six-mile walk together. Every Christmas Eve we would shop for a Northwest seafood dinner that the family would eat after church that night. Now that she's an adult, I am so thankful we did those daddy-daughter things. They have definitely helped build a strong relationship.

96

Rotate responsibilities with each of them.

At bedtime, Patty and I would rotate who would put which child to bed each night. The kids got to spend dedicated time with each of us during their bedtime routine. Briana and I had our little things only she and I would do, like reading *Ranger Rick* magazine at bedtime.

97

Do things with all of them.

We all four love watching movies and can quote lines from movies such as *How the Grinch Stole Christmas* ("Stay Focused!"), *Mrs. Doubtfire* ("Hellllooooooo!"), *Aladdin* ("BEEEE Yourself!") and *A Christmas Story* (Fra-GEE-lay!). Now that the kids are adults, they still love to rattle off movie lines. We love it too.

The Journey Doesn't End, it Changes

98

Provide a safe environment for advice.

The evening we left Trevor at his dorm room we had a discussion over dinner about soliciting advice. We told him, "For small decisions, get advice from one person you trust, for big decisions, get advice from three people you trust." Four weeks later we were on the phone with him and he asked our advice about something. We gave it to him and he said, "See I had a small decision and asked your advice." Loved it.

99

Leverage your job as a coach.

We have been very deliberate with Trevor about letting him know that Patty and I are now planning to do less parenting and more coaching with him. This reinforces a number of concepts: he is an adult and is responsible for his own decisions; we are there for him; he gets to decide what advice to take; and he is accountable for the outcome of his decisions.

100

Never stop saying I love you.

Some fathers have difficulty expressing this to anyone, especially their kids. Every time we talk with Trevor or Briana I make it a point to tell them that we love them very much. It's not only important for them to hear it, it's important for me to say it and remind myself what a wonderful son and daughter we've been blessed with.

Citations:

Lessons 1-8 – Center for Disease Control - http://www.cdc.gov/ncbddd/autism/

See the entire Six-Word Lesson Series at
6wordlessons.com

Want to learn more about Autism?
Check out *GrowingUpAutistic.com*

Read more about the author at
LonniePacelli.com

Made in the USA
San Bernardino, CA
14 November 2013